WHAT IS MONEY?

KATIE MARSICO

Published in the United States of America by Cherry Lake Publishing
Ann Arbor, Michigan
www.cherrylakepublishing.com

Math Education: Dr. Timothy Whiteford, Associate Professor of Education at St. Michael's College
Financial Adviser: Kenneth Klooster, financial adviser at Edward Jones Investments
Reading Adviser: Marla Conn, ReadAbility, Inc.

Photo Credits: © Thinkstock Images, cover, 1; © Lost Mountain Studio/Shutterstock Images, 5; © Baiploo/Shutterstock Images, 6; © Henrryk Sadura/Shutterstock Images, 9; © Ragnarock/Shutterstock Images, 10; © GWImages/Shutterstock Images, 12; © fstop123/iStock.com, 15; © Samuel Borges Photography/Shutterstock Images, 16; © Pincasso/Shutterstock Images, 19; © jcjphotography/Shutterstock Images, 20; © bopav/Shutterstock Images, 23; © Andrew Scherbackov/Shutterstock Images, 25; © Fentino/iStock.com, 27; © Warren Price Photography/Shutterstock Images, 29

Library of Congress Cataloging-in-Publication Data

Marsico, Katie, 1980-
    What is money? / Katie Marsico.
  pages cm. — (Real world math: personal finance)
  Includes bibliographical references and index.
  ISBN 978-1-63362-579-2 (hardcover) — ISBN 978-1-63362-759-8 (pdf) — ISBN 978-1-63362-669-0 (pbk.) — ISBN 978-1-63362-849-6 (ebook)
  1. Money—Juvenile literature. 2. Finance, Personal—Mathematics—Juvenile literature. I. Title.

  HG221.5.M335 2016
  332.4—dc23   2015008969

Cherry Lake Publishing would like to acknowledge the work of the Partnership for 21st Century Skills. Please visit *www.p21.org* for more information.

Printed in the United States of America
Corporate Graphics

ABOUT THE AUTHOR

Katie Marsico is the author of more than 200 children's books. She lives in a suburb of Chicago, Illinois, with her husband and children.

TABLE OF CONTENTS

Rocks, Corn, and Salt

Have you ever received money as a gift? Maybe it was in the form of a gift card for an online retailer such as iTunes. If you lived thousands of years ago, the "money" you received would probably have been rocks or shells!

In ancient times, people exchanged goods for other goods or services. For example, a bushel of corn was sometimes **bartered**, or traded, for a bushel of potatoes.

But bartering frequently grew complicated. After all, how many bushels of wheat should be traded for a cow? People began using **currency**, or money, to put an actual value on a product.

People used to trade food for other food they wanted, instead of paying for it with money.

Coins have been around for thousands of years.

Money in ancient times didn't always look like today's money. Blocks of salt, barley, beads, and feathers were all ancient forms of currency. Some people think that the first coins came from the ancient kingdom of Lydia, which is now Turkey. Other people believe that the first coins were made in China thousands of years ago.

The Chinese also began using paper money, which was much lighter than coins. The government printed pieces of paper called receipts. Special designs were used so no one could copy the paper. Each receipt had a fixed value. Later, early European settlers to the United States brought coins from many different countries. They often traded with Native Americans. Native American money was made of shells, called wampum, woven into belts and bracelets.

The British government did not allow the colonists to print their own money. They had to use a combination of coins, wampum, and goods to buy and sell products. After the colonists declared their independence, they created money for the new United States. How was this money developed? Who creates all the money today?

21ST CENTURY CONTENT

As time passed, many countries created unique coins. They were made of gold, silver, copper, and bronze. Some were round. Others were square. Chinese coins were round with a square hole in the middle! Ancient coins featured symbols and images of animals and rulers. Why was it important that coins from different countries had their own special designs?

Making Money

In 1782, the newly formed U.S. government created the first U.S. Mint in Philadelphia, Pennsylvania. A mint is where coins are made. Today, **circulating** coins are also minted in Denver, Colorado.

Certain words and expressions must appear on circulating coins. These are "Liberty," "In God We Trust," "United States of America," and *E Pluribus Unum* (which is Latin for "out of many, one"). Each coin also displays its **denomination** and the year it was minted.

So, how are coins designed and developed? First, an

artist creates a design that must be approved by the U.S. Congress. Next, a plastic model of the coin is created. A machine copies the design from the plastic coin onto a small metal die. A die is a device used for shaping objects. In a separate machine, sheets of metal are cut

Coins are made at the U.S. Mint in Denver, Colorado.

American paper bills are mostly green and white, but bills from other countries are different colors.

into disks. These disks, called blanks, are heated, cooled, cleaned, and shaped. The dies are put inside a machine called a coin press. A coin is minted when this machine presses the dies into the blanks. Each press creates 750 new coins a minute! Finally, the coins are bagged, weighed, and stored until distributed.

In 1861, the U.S. Treasury began printing paper money. Today, paper currency in the United States includes denominations of $1, $2, $5, $10, $20, $50, and $100. The Bureau of Engraving and Printing is responsible for printing all U.S. paper currency. Money is printed in Washington, D.C., and Fort Worth, Texas.

Different countries produce different forms of currency. For example, Canadians don't have $1 or $2 bills. Instead, they use a $1 coin called a loonie and a $2 coin called a toonie.

In the United States, the paper for U.S. currency is made up of a special blend of cotton and linen. Red and blue fibers are included in the blend. The average life of a $5 bill is about five years. In comparison, the average life of most coins is approximately 30 years.

REAL WORLD MATH CHALLENGE

You've probably heard the expression a "ton of money." A ton of pennies = $3,630.00. A ton of quarters = $40,000.00. A ton of $1 bills = $908,000.00.

- How many pennies are in a ton?
- How many quarters are in a ton?
- How many more $1 bills should be added to a ton to increase its value to $1 million?

(Turn to page 30 for the answers)

These are just a few of the many American state quarter designs.

21ST CENTURY CONTENT

In 2003, the U.S. Mint launched the Artistic Infusion Program (AIP). As part of AIP, artists apply for the chance to design the 50 state quarters. The quarters have icons that represent each state's landscape and culture. In 2010, they began a second set, with designs of landmarks, and this will be completed in 2021. Each year, different artists are added as others leave the program. It's an innovative way of creating new career options for artists. Who designed your state's quarter?

Workers at mints are aware that it's easier to copy paper money than coins. Sometimes, dishonest people try to create **counterfeit** money. It looks like the real thing but has no value. If you study a bill, you'll see many safeguards that indicate it's real money. Each bill has a special **serial number** and a Treasury seal. In addition, security threads make it more difficult to copy the paper with a color copier. Finally, the U.S. Treasury adds changes to the bills every 7 to 10 years. These changes also make it harder to copy U.S. currency.

Now you know about the history of money and how it's produced. Next, let's look at how math makes those pieces of metal and paper so valuable!

CHAPTER 3

Do the Math: Why Money Has Value

What if a neighbor hired you to shovel snow but offered to pay you in seashells instead of cash? Seashells have no value at a store. Money is valuable because you're able to use it to purchase goods and services. Stores accept your money and use it to purchase items and pay employees. Workers use the money they earn to buy things from other stores. They also deposit money in the bank for future purchases. All of this is part of our **economic system**.

Banks manage their accounts, but who manages the

banks? In 1913, Congress created the Federal Reserve System. The purpose of the "Fed" is to provide a stable **monetary** system for U.S. money. It's like a bank for the other banks, and the bank for our government.

By going shopping, people influence the economic system around them.

The best time to buy a car is when your interest rates will be low.

One job of the Fed is to keep interest rates low. Interest rates are what you pay when you borrow money. If interest rates are low, borrowers are able to pay off their debts while only paying a small amount of interest money. When interest rates are high, borrowers end up paying a lot of interest money.

The actual value of the dollar can change over time. Such changes are caused by **inflation** and **deflation**. Inflation happens when the demand for an item goes up but the supply goes down. Deflation is the opposite. For example, in 1930, you could buy a loaf of bread for about $0.09. By 1967, that price had jumped to about $0.22. In the 1990s, it was around $1.00. These days, in 2015, a loaf of bread can be anywhere from $2.00 to $4.50, depending on its ingredients and where it's made. Did the prices jump overnight? No—inflation usually happens over a long period of time. Inflation and deflation are important in determining the value of money in our economy.

REAL WORLD MATH CHALLENGE

Joseph borrowed $60.00 from his brother Mike. Joseph agrees to pay Mike $20.00 a week plus 3 percent interest weekly on the balance of the loan until it's repaid.

- How long will it take Joseph to repay his loan?
- How much interest will Joseph pay each week?
- How much total interest will Joseph pay? Calculate interest before subtracting each week's payment.

(Turn to page 30 for the answers)

Do the Math: Kinds of Money

When banks first began using paper notes, or bills, the money represented actual gold or silver. Anyone could go to a bank in the United States and trade paper money for gold or silver. It was called the gold standard.

Today, however, our money is called **fiat money**. The currency we use is considered to be legal trade by our government. A paper bill itself has no value. The value of the money comes from supply and demand.

Another kind of money is credit. With credit, you purchase a product but promise to pay for it in the future—typically with interest. People also make purchases using bank loans. Short-term loans, such as credit card purchases, are generally used to pay for a variety of everyday items. They tend to have higher interest rates than bank loans. Meanwhile, bank loans

A home buyer will usually need to take out a loan to afford the purchase.

When you deposit a check, the bank will take money from the check writer's account and put it into yours.

are often used to pay for more expensive items such as homes or cars. They usually feature lower interest rates because they're repaid over a longer period of time.

You're also able to buy and sell products and services with checks and electronic transfers. Imagine that your friend Laura sells you her Rollerblades. You write Laura a check. A check is a written promise from you that a business or person will receive money in the amount that the check states.

Laura deposits it in her bank account. Your bank

[21ST CENTURY SKILLS LIBRARY]

deducts the amount from your account and sends it to Laura's bank, where it is deposited in her account. This is called an electronic money transfer.

Gift cards are another type of currency. When you receive a gift card, someone has already prepaid a set amount on the card for you. You're able to use this money to shop at whatever store or restaurant is listed on the card. For example, Amazon.com sells gift cards that allow you to purchase everything from books to music online.

REAL WORLD MATH CHALLENGE

Julie has a $25.00 Amazon.com gift card. She's already bought 17 digital songs that cost $0.99 each. Now she wants to buy her favorite book for her Kindle. The book costs $8.85.

- How much of the gift card has Julie already spent?
- Does she have enough left for the book?
- If not, how much more money will she need?

(Turn to page 30 for the answers)

We've learned about money in the United States, but foreign currency is also important. We live in a global economy. The value of currency in one country has an impact on the value of currency in another. The value of one country's money in a different country is called the exchange rate. At one point in 2015, $1.00 of American currency equaled approximately $1.26 of Canadian currency. The exchange rate varies from country to country and changes frequently.

21ST CENTURY CONTENT

In the late 1990s, the governments of several European countries worked together to achieve a more stable economy. Instead of each nation having its own money, they all decided to use the same currency—the euro. The euro is now used in countries such as Italy, Spain, Portugal, and France. What do you think are some advantages of this system?

Exchange rates change often, but usually in very small amounts each time.

CHAPTER 5

Make Your Money Count for You!

If you think the money you spend doesn't make a difference in our economic system, think again. There are millions of kids your age in the United States. Many of them spend hundreds of dollars of their own money each year. That adds up to billions of dollars going into our economy. Making good shopping choices not only helps you, it helps the economy, too.

It is important to start practicing good math and money management skills now. They will give you the tools you need to have a better financial future. The best place to begin is with a plan. A plan to keep track of your money is called a budget. A budget should include your assets (income) and expenditures (expenses). Start by keeping a journal of your expenses for a few weeks.

Learning how to keep track of your money when you're young can save you a lot of trouble when you're older.

LIFE AND CAREER SKILLS

People are constantly using technology to find new and exciting ways to create and exchange money. For example, some bank customers deposit money by simply snapping a photo of a check with their smartphone. Next, they send this electronic image to the bank, and presto—a deposit is made!

Write down everything. Keeping track of your money helps you see what your greatest expenditures are.

Learn to tell the difference between wants and needs. Before you make a purchase, stop and ask yourself if you *need* this item or simply *want* it. It's also possible to use the money you have to make more money. Banks will pay you interest on the money you keep in a savings account. People often earn interest on other **investments**, too. To figure out how fast you'll be able to double your money, use the "Rule of 72." Simply take 72, and divide it by the interest rate. The answer is the approximate number of years it will take to double your original amount of money.

These days, lots of smartphone apps can help you manage your money.

Money has evolved in many different ways throughout history. Salt and shells have been replaced by electronic transfers and credit cards. What hasn't changed is the practice of exchanging something of value for something you want or need. How are you spending or saving your money today?

REAL WORLD MATH CHALLENGE

Mrs. Garcia carefully tracks her expenses. She notices that the price of milk is increasing. In the past four months, she paid $2.45, $2.60, $2.75, and $2.90.

- What is the difference between each months' prices?
- Based on this, what do you predict the cost will be in the fifth month?
- How much will the price of milk have increased during this five-month period?

(Turn to page 30 for the answers)

Years ago, some Native Americans used wampum beads as their form of money.

Real World Math Challenge Answers

CHAPTER TWO
Page 11
There are 363,000 pennies in a ton.
3,630 ÷ $.01 = 363,000

There are 160,000 quarters in a ton.
40,000 ÷ $.25 = 160,000

Exactly 92,000 more $1 bills should be added to a ton to increase its value to $1 million.
$1,000,000.00 − $908,000.00 = $92,000.00

CHAPTER THREE
Page 17
It will take Joseph 3 weeks to repay his loan.
$60.00 ÷ $20.00 = 3 weeks

Joseph will pay Mike $1.80 in interest the first week.
$60.00 x 0.03 interest = $1.80
After the first week, Joseph's balance is $40.00.
$60.00 − $20.00 = $40.00

Joseph will pay Mike $1.20 in interest the second week.
$40.00 x 0.03 = $1.20
After the second week, Joseph's balance is $20.00.
$40.00 − $20.00 = $20.00

Joseph will pay Mike $0.60 in interest the third and final week.
$20.00 x 0.03 = $0.60

Joseph will pay $3.60 in total interest.
$1.80 + $1.20 + $0.60 = $3.60

CHAPTER FOUR
Page 21
Julie has already spent $16.83 of the gift card.
17 songs x $0.99 each = $16.83

She does not have enough left for the book.
$25.00 − $16.83 = $8.17

She'll need $0.68 more.
$8.85 − $8.17 = $0.68

CHAPTER FIVE
Page 28
The difference between the prices each month is $0.15.
$2.60 − $2.45 = $0.15
$2.75 − $2.60 = $0.15
$2.90 − $2.75 = $0.15

Based on this, the predicted cost next month will be $3.05.
$2.90 + $0.15 = $3.05

The price of milk will have increased $0.60 in total.
$0.15 + $0.15 + $0.15 + $0.15 = $0.60

Find Out More

BOOKS

Jenkins, Martin, and Satoshi Kitamura (illustrator). *The History of Money: From Bartering to Banking*. Somerville, MA: Candlewick Press, 2014.

Marsico, Katie. *Money Math*. Minneapolis: Lerner Publications, 2016.

Thompson, Helen. *Banking Math*. Broomall, PA: Mason Crest Publishers, 2013.

WEB SITES

Kids.gov—Money
www.kids.gov/k_5/k_5_money.shtml
Learn more about the money-making process and counterfeit currency.

Royal Canadian Mint—Curious About Coins?
http://www.mint.ca/store/content/htmlTemplate.jsp?cat=Kids%27+Corner&nId=100 000&nodeGroup=Learn#.VRRjh_ldXTo
Find out more about how Canadian coins are made.

Treasury Direct—Kids
https://www.treasurydirect.gov/kids/kids.htm
Watch videos, play games, and read fun facts about the U.S. Department of Treasury.

GLOSSARY

bartered (BAR-turd) traded products, goods, or services instead of using money

circulating (SUR-kyoo-late-ing) objects such as coins that are in the state of being passed from person to person

counterfeit (KOUN-tur-fit) made to look like something else in order to deceive

currency (KUR-uhn-see) money in circulation that is used in a particular country

deflation (di-FLAY-shuhn) a general price decrease for goods and services

denomination (di-nom-uh-NAY-shuhn) the value of a single bill or coin

economic system (ek-uh-NOM-ik SISS-tuhm) the production, distribution, and consumption of goods and services

fiat money (FEE-it MUH-nee) paper currency that cannot be exchanged for gold or silver

inflation (in-FLAY-shuhn) a general price increase for goods and services

investments (in-VEST-muhntz) financial efforts that involve spending money in the hopes of ultimately making a profit

monetary (MON-uh-tair-ee) relating to money

serial number (SIHR-ee-uhl NUM-bur) a unique number given to each bill of currency to help prevent counterfeiting

INDEX